BIOCHEMICAL

A Strangers Testimony

Vidar Hebek

ISBN 978-82-690224-4-5

Prelude

And the light shines
in the darkness
and the darkness
did not comprehend it.
John 1.5

Psalm Seven Eleven

(Over There)

Welcome to America.
God save the country.
Wicked as you are.
Countdown with firecrackers
countdown with the proudness.
Wicked as we are.
God save America
and we believe it
no more jokes, and no
more food.
Welcome to America.

And God is angry
with the wicked
every day.

          Psalm 7.11

Gospel

Go ahead, I will do it.
Trust me, so I will.
The Cross was for you.
Believe it or not.
In His blood
you were.
So be aware.
You can be lost
in vain.
And do not
Say
Amen.

Light bearer

My name is
Lucifer
my name is
many.
The father of
all lies
shaken but not stirred.

Sly but not silly
light bulb
for all
liars.
Come on
let me be
your shining
angel.

And you will look
like
a righteous one.

When you are
not
scared anymore
you are
an easy target.

Dazzle of eyes

Block the door
no entrance.
Passing by
I am
waiting
can you see.

Blurred eye
do not go
anywhere.
Vision and beyond
is only
for members.

Do you think
you are
able
to reach it?

Anywhere in
the world
music is stretching
out
to a star.

And beyond
it is ringing
a bell.

Star Wars

Ku Klux Clan
is not the one
who pull the trigger.
Ungodliness do
the job
nobody wants.

Return to Hell
is easy
when you
give glory
to your desire.

On the
Dark side
of the moon
you find an
Ocean of
wilderness
and you say:
Could we have
some more.

California beach

(Eureka; ancient Greek word; "I have found
(it)")

Wave after waves
same direction
but unstable
in all their
ways.
Communication will
always follow
a stranger.

Testimony is
when you have been
stranded
on a beach
and have
something
to tell.

The question is
who listens
except
those who
were stranded.

An end time story

A message
which is not
told
before it is
too late.

A crusade for
the lost one
(whom) you find
in an island
which is not
there anymore.

Cry out
for more
nowhere to
hide, a story
is already
told, and crying
out loud
have a deeper
meaning.

Hypocrites!

Actor under an
assumed character
Oscar for
best performance.
A picture within
subjects which (is/are)
no longer
there.
And everybody
wants them.

The true color
can turn grey
and the subjects
is risen to
a high level.
Communication is only
for those
who know
what all is
about.
And do not lift
a finger.

Tiller of the ground

To weep over
our sin
to spend time
and to fertilizing
the ground
you are
married to.

Who beat who?
Who had an
eye to see?

Cain killed Abel
for what
reason?
Can anyone
do the same
for
what reason?
Except being
tiller of the ground.

Man on the moon

The earth circulates
around
the sun
I wonder
what sun
does, since
it obviously moving
also.

With my eyes
I can see
even from distance.
When distance makes you
comfortable, and your
surroundings is closer
than it looks
and my point
of view
and DreamWorks
seen from a
distance
makes the Man
on the Moon
little bit
different.

Closer I look
it seems
I have to start
all over again.

The Son of Man

The moon is
silent, only some
footsteps left.

Shall we continue;
the Word was
in the beginning
and the Word was
God.
Unbelievable that
faith took over
no doubt
seems so far
away.

By Word
He put everything
right, even
Black holes
which we could not
put the finger on
even if we
try.
What is left is
that the Word
was
with God.

When the law had risen

Ten Commandments
makes the rock
stable.
Broken in two
makes my
mother
unstable, force
from strongholds
makes the atmosphere
foggy.

Life comes
when you fail
and broken finger
from those who
pointing on
you.
When you regret
is that the Law
had risen.

When it comes to an end

Revolution from
sin
declares that
the path is
narrow.
Wide is
those who
have
lost the destination.

Rock and roll
tells you
something else.
Sex will open
up your
mind.
And drugs
keep it
going.

Save the wisdom
for later
and fearing
God
is for foreigners
and strangers
who walk
to an end.

Imagine

Imagine
there is Hell
below.

Imagine
there is a song
which is from
the wicked one.

Imagine
there is a lie
we believe in it.

Imagine
that I am
a dreamer
and not the only
one.

Imagine
that Hell is real
and we are
lost in space.

Imagine
that we are
in space
and we have
occupied it.

Imagine
there is a Heaven
above us (Over There)
and no one
believes in it.

Imagine
there is One
who stretches out
His hand
and everyone
rejected it.

Imagine
I sing a song
no one listens
to
and the melody is
silent.

Broken glasses

Broken glasses
is: Made in
China.
Quality is perfection
made of
a product
is clear to
see.

Clearness
is made of
pureness.
Widows recover
and orphans is
not alone.
To be
unspotted from
this world
will make
your quality
famous.

Go ahead
rise your hand
and you will
make it.

Glorifying
the product
set me in
a production
which someone
can
copy it.

All rights reserved

Forbidden words
do not tell anyone
and miracles happen.

Cosmos is created
by His hand
and words:
Let there be
light.

In the light
we saw
something closer
to our eyes.

And eyes took
control over what
is left, and signify
for themselves
all rights
like kicking the leg
of Goliath without
allowance.

And creator versus
creature, could likely
be
all rights reserved
and human knowledge
become an
assumed character.

Arrogance

Mount Everest is
higher than
my self.

Pulpit is
my arrogance
when I
reach to the
top.
And climbing
a tree
is more easier.

Specially when
you are
able to look
down at
people
far away.

The Nature
has nothing
to do with
it.
Except to
survive
our own
arrogance.

Aliens

My lips are
sealed
even with
open mouth.

Gospel is told
without words
and imagination
do not
exist.
And I am
a little flower
which learn to
speak.

Grammar takes me
everywhere I wish
and bend me
down
where grass is
green, and
girls are pretty.

Imagination brings me
closer to
my truth, and itching
ears, is what
I like to
hear.

Fragrance of the oil

Ignore the society
glorifying what is
mine, the smell of
riches, confusion
when everyone
think you are
the cause.

To be anointed
by the poor
smell of fragrance
make the rich
amazed, and hindrance
to receive what
is a value.

Pumping up
darkness which the
smell of biochemical
fragrance, made in
disorder.

The anointed oil
and character have
an another value.

Over there

The normal way
is craziness
in God's eyes.

Glorifying Big Bang
which takes me
further out
in Space, and
including everyone else.

Craziness denies
that something is
made of nothing.

And nothing
takes me
further in
to an emptiness
I never thought
I had.

And blinking of
an eye
normalize
the point of view.

Over the brook

Crossing is easy
lift your hand
do not think
your challenge
will be easier.

Drowning is deeper
than your angle
and free will
is hard.
And fighting
on the other
side
makes it, complicated.

To wrestle with
God
and be
blessed
rather that, than
against an
enemy, and rivers
which can take
you
anywhere.

A map

Direction.
East, west
up and down
whatever
wherever
and distance
is multiplied
with mass.

To look far
needs Energy
divided by
the speed of
the light, sunshine
makes it clear
and pollution
inside an
understanding.

And distance equals
direction multiplied
with speed of light
divided on my
lack of statement
when it comes
to maps.

Atmosphere

Harden your heart
and make the
idols come true
in your hand.

Walk on line
put everything
right. Smooth and
soft, like
air.
Before ice
and temperature
is rising.
Except you.

Is it empty
when breathing
in every
circumstances and
sinking with
mouth shut
and desperately
try to
scream out
some tears.

Beyond the time

Blinded by the
light, beyond
the root of
a second.
Energy equal
mass, multiply
with speed of
light. And prosperity
can be
too much.

Lack of
nothing, said
it too many
times, and disappear
out of an
universe. And inside
a skull, where
the dimension
is smaller.

And astronauts
who try to
get into
something less.
Blinded by the
feelings of being
nowhere.

Ignorance

Platform of mortal
arrogance. Simplicity
and empty space.
Blessed are those
(who are)
poor in spirit, and
acknowledge of
something more.

And platform which
is fully
booked, not able
to reach any
quantum of solace. Made
up an idea, and
created by
themselves.

Ignorance do things
to you, to
you, more space
makes it
empty. And what
I know, is
the least thing
I can
do.

Threshold

When you enter
a limit for
an arena, private
but open agenda.
Passover for
evil propaganda.
Nothing less
nothing more.

A limit for
understanding
in what is
mine. Property
on the other
side. And opinion
have two sides
with a door
locked.

It is a
space between
living and
knocking.
Who will open
is only a
matter of
a question.

Firstborn

Translate the oldest
which will be
the last.
Common sense
do things to
you.
And stubbornness.

And the last
will be
the first in
moment of Firstborn.
Promised land
before earthquake and
desert.
Crowded and lonely
made of nothing, will
find you in the
surroundings.

Beware of zero
times billions is
nothing to
declare. But
sacrifices of One
of billions.
And last will
be the first.

Redeem

If someone
knocking the
entrance for
disturbing, a door
between you and
me, salesmen
you reject, neighbors
which will not
listening. Only
have your door
open.

Release yourself
from yourself.
Destiny is to
find, lost part.
And do the
work, stand up
and open
your mind.

When Christ is
knocking your door
the key word
will be opened
from inside.
Pure love
wipe out
tears you did
not thought you
have.
And all in
your mind
is redeemed.

On the Edge

I want to
get out
and live
on the edge
which becomes
crowded, and only
way back
is repentance.

To have a
dream
and nightmare
is when I
wake up.

I am
one of them
who rather
have my fingers
burnt
than see the sign
of: Warning.

And true believers
Just
Do it.

Lot's wife

Every step I
take and past
is not even
a future.
The mind
can reject it
with light of
speed.
Forth or back
is what I
choose.

Do not look
back, it is simple
and have it
revealed; is a custom.
Foreigners longing
home, prisoners wishing
they did not
do what is
done, and grammar
help me
a lot.

Symbolize the mind
and parallels of
feet walking
on water with
faith on global
pressure of
gravity.

Anatomy

Life is way
too short to
live it.
It ringing a bell
before timeout
never ending
story of fortune.
Indicate true access
of the dust
right before I straighten
my back and honor
the authority, way beyond
my understanding.

Low standard is
overweight, too much
circumstances. And my
skeleton are suddenly
out of order.
And also the last
which disappear into
soil. From dust
to fertilizer, and
something revealed; it is
too late.

Armor of God

To shoot him
who have killed
make sense
for tiller of
the ground.
My own
justice need
to proclaim what
is right.
And to miss
the mark is
sin.

Against principalities
against powers
which rules on
what is obvious
weight of gold.
Armor means
I am
in war.

Appearance

Short hair, long
hair. Design colored
from grey. Old
to young. Spirit of
fear. And then
pension.

Land after
bombing, laser
for measure
the mess in
your face. Sympathy
for the devil
and the cruel
world.

Concrete make
faces soft, until
you stop
smiling, and crying
for the loss
from hair
on shoulder
which is able
to carry
a head without
any logic.

Lyrics

Tsunami takes you
further in and
out. Left behind
is an another
picture. Develop
a wall does
not help. A tribune
of acknowledgement.

Poems sound
ridiculous in
stereo, brings you
further and further
anywhere it want.

Try to be
clever, make you
poor in spirit.
First then it
will become
reasonable.
Lyrics speak
another
language, like
God.

Airborne

Speed limit
before it expire.
Hurry if you can.
No troubled
autostrada. Highway
to Hell, write
a letter is faster
these days. Solid
as it is.

Mobile is comfort
satellite catch
up miracles, radio signal
is sensitive these
days, and travel
in First Class.
Past memorize
present legalize everything.
Future gives birth
to sin; and sin
brings forth death.

From Tropical
to places where
coldness is an
language, injected
blood samples and everyone
is equal. Sun
goes down, spiritual
it means; wake
up before
it is too late.

Cargo for deliverance
above the world
which is under the evil.

Dancing Tango

Someone to blame
mixture of the world
sweet and sour.
I am the last
to see myself.
Expression are dialogue
after sunset and
even millionaire is
left behind.
Someone to blame?

Miracles happen
said it
before, once more
and that is it.
Did it my
way, and Hell is
near, stamping
on feet, no rhythm
but miracle happens.

It takes two
night and day
arguing of
who started. Sunset
is not The End.
It just started
and it takes two.

Resistance

Plural agreement
common sense
when someone dies.
Red and white
resistance in your
blood, fighting for
right to
party.

Live to die
die to live
make sense
only for those
who are single.
One and Only.

The Blood poured
out for you
showing us
darkness, before
sunrise, and resistance
before sunset.

False witness

Shining angels
darkness in eyes
comes from heart
to mouth and evil
thoughts, which is
open for anyone
a mall open
for everyone
except God.

Did you point
your fingers
hold back the
truth, and is it
me you talking
about, what to
say? Maybe
you have right
except God.

Waiting for the
hour, when I am
ready to be
a false witness
which I thought
I was not
included in my
heart, except
God Almighty.

Reach the Top

Climbing up
a failure down
reaching heights
and fear of heights
for those who
are under beneath.

Wish you were
here, point of
view, fare
enough is
enough. I am
always out
to the horizon
and further
killing me
softly, and lack
of faith
travels into
the impossible.

Prospect to much
to little, and reach
the Top is
nothing left.
Except glorifying
myself
right before
I vanish
away, just like
a flower.

Evolution

What ever you read
believe it.
Monkey to human.
Nothing to something.
Someone to everyone.
Ism to Ism.
From lies to lies
many times enough
until you
believe it
and take it
as a truth.

Confusion leads blind
and let them
play, sooner or
later someone
kicking some sand
in their eyes.
Blind leads
blind, into
ditch and then
the childhood
was over.

Copycat

Devil, Diabolos;
accuser, splitter, evil
speaker and father
of all lies.
Turn out to be
a shining angel
or light if you
wish.

Short memory
dialogue with the lost
false prophet, religious
imposter, many will
deceive many, multiplied
is pretty many.

Stand by me
with a nice voice
singing a song
and itching ears
which it is
pretty many.

A producer of
death, and he
is not your
friend.
But let us talk
about Love
finally.

Greatest of them all

How can I
write about
Love
if I do not
have any?
Hollywood do
the same, an
error of assumed
character.

Turn my back.
Love my enemy
make myself
more friends.
Hospitality brings
me out.
Heart is more
than blood.
And try to
save
my life
is death.

Love endures
all things, but
did not
comprehend it.
To grow cold
means; I
actually had it.
Love make no
sense, when I
do not have
it.

Vengeance

Twin Tower
is two of
a kind.
Revenge is
turning the
other cheek.
A tooth for a tooth
and you loose
booth, and love
your enemy
so start
with yourself.

Revenge does
the world
not so
crowded anymore.
Distance make
the people
to start
all over again.
And pray
for those
who persecute you.

Proverbs for
fools, wisdom
and understanding
will knock
your head of.
And vengeance
is not for
new beginners.

Islamic

The vengeance is
mine
says the Lord.
One who lived
long enough
to see
someone mooned
their butt
to idols.
Respect are
rootless, unless
it is based
on facts.

False prophet
religious imposter:
I will repay
says the Lord.
Shining Angels
look a like.
And deceive
many.

Love endures
all things.
A righteous man
avails much.
Darkness did not
comprehend it.
Because they could
be blinded by
The Light.

Jesus Christ

I died once
from everything
still alive
but not
 as before.

Everything that creeps
under the skin
when I wake up
and look
back.

Trickle the water
in the same way
the time I died
and live
more than ever.

Miracle

To divide
in two
what is the problem
cells
do the same.
In fact, so must
something be splitted
to move on
further.

Divide
to become
a people
we can fight against.

Red Sea
has been
world famous
no one believes in
why not
could they only
walk on water.

Social

The Lightning said
to Thunder; let me
be allowed to come
first
since I am
faster than you.

The Thunder said
to the Lightning; let me get
allowed to bother
most
so I also
can make me
noticed.

My little head

Clamped
in a existence
my little
head
extends
out to
microcosm
further did I
not come.

Paralyzed
have something to do
with the eyes
like sand
in the wind.
And you do not know
where it
comes from.

Could it not
just get big
enough.
To wander
right through.

Fleeing through
universe
and existence
have something to do with
numbers, a calculation
of dimensions.
And then
I is
just a flower.

Chameleon

I fit in
everywhere, behind
a period it is
all over again.
Climate, colors
twilight adjusting
my senses to
impress circumstances
in time of
age. And I
am open
for everything.

Made to be
human, in an
image which
fits in.
Hide and seek
is my
destiny.

The Fall of Man
made the fear
as my weapon
and protection.
Sincere is when
I live up
to it.
And die
with it.

No identity

Are you ready
for renewal
keep the exchange
do the work of
a laborer and
inherit what belongs
to an employer
what is taken
is given.

What is given
is taken on
behalf of what
was given, to
no man, no woman
unless a tree
rooted by the
brook. Exceedingly
it make it
grow. And blooming
is an another
language.

Pureness after
cleaning, and the
subject is mine.
Object is what
to see, and object
without subject is
nothing, and nothing
comes from nothing.
Familiar but far
from understanding.
And nothing to
declare.

Solomon

My Father is
greater than your
father. A childhood
lack of wisdom
but pure
energy, and understanding
of danger
from falling in
dreams and
it never end.

Acknowledge comes
from burnt
finger pointing
on you. Disharmony
desire, disobedient
idols, and so on
and so on.

Vanity of vanities
all is vanity.
Basement of all
anxiety, it takes one
to know one.
To search is
to dig deeper
and made it
solid, not able
to rock.

Confusion

Expand or die.
Misery for the
people, but who
cares. Emperor do
their homework.
Stagnate and die.
Life put to
death, blood poured
out, and everything
is yours.

Insurance cover
all things
except accident
and coincidence.
Who to blame
when you hear
another language
inside a territory
peeing on someones
tree. Babel to
blame, and we try
to scatter them
over the face
of all the
earth.

Holy Spirit

Stagnate and become
lukewarm, climate
chancing, so do you.
Primate or predator.
Simplicity or complicated.
Landscape or wilderness.
Heaven or earth
or both.

Spring is burning
out their leaves.
Love does not
grow cold, but
fire of life.
To make my self
clear, and you
know that
I am clear.
Speak the truth
and die.

Branches of The One
His offspring
to life, from
nothing in you.
An atmosphere of
atom and molecule.
Blinded by the eyes
but still there.
And the Wind.

A blink of an eye

Are you with
me or against
the opportunity
to see a face
feet walking on water
who forgive
and blessing the
children. And never
give up.

Landslide, volcanos
and like, invisible
but in the News
feelings turned of
with remote control.
And that is it.

So come on
baby, let us Dance
seduce my mind.
Then something
above blinking
His eye. Sooner
the better.
And that is it.

Access

You wanna go
all the way
in, code security
secrets above
revelation does not
comes alone
grab it
like Carpe Diem.

Computers have
secrets and He
who sees
all things, digitals
is number, in mathematics
order, and plenty
is advanced.

Software is an
idol, paid in
advanced metallic
sound. Password is
forgiveness, humbleness
repentance and a sound
mind.

Falling down

Feeling kills
gravity helps.
Prosperity rise
up dignity
dignity is
self-defense on
everything that
moves, and continue
falling in
dreams.

Sanctify yourself
walk out, get
into it, pureness
help a lot, again
and again, repeat
not forget, word
is pieces, swallow
one, lose your breath
and you are
there.

Single man and
woman, who wants
to be distracted.
Their pulpit is
larger than them.
And falling down
is an
expression.

Paper work

Heavenly signature.
Mark my word.
Loud and clear
with an exclamation mark.
Question mark is for
devil and his
minions. Herald His
name and be
quiet.

Clarify a period
before you start
to finished and
fulfill your race.
And figure how
much it will
cost you.

Book of paper
by inspiration of God.
Not spirit of
fear, but power
and sound mind.
World comes around
energy equal mass
and gravity divided
by itself.

Dignity

Melancholy kill
music in ear
and where does it
end. And melody
make us crying
in pictures of
an Colosseum. Mass
equal energy
feelings multiplied with
itself.

I am not
here, to fearful
anxiety kills, sooner
than doctrines, in
a head which
you can not
catch but is
there.

Fear as rock
do not fear
grammar open
up for
everything. Lost
in space, talk for
itself. Inside
a skull.

Seminar

Dead blood smells
blood cries out
from the ground.
Seminar for similar
people, who have
no place to
terminate their pain.
And in weekends
is nothing to do.

Seminar for those
who have no
accountancy in life
no goal to hit
the target of
anyone is war.
To many is beginning
of less.

Seminar for speculation
you never know
a day to die
a lifetime to learn
which is short
memory from past.
Remembrance is the
beginning of all
knowledge. Wisdom is
something else.

Revelation

Horizon of what
is beyond, vision
have not happened
yet. Space beyond
present. Time before
although, roaming with
what we see
and eyes is an
hindrance in
vision and beyond.

Consider this
kick Goliath in
his leg, tribulation
darkness and sober
stars. Soak in
be there, revelation
of The world
going under. Secret
is told
and not
there.

Way under, prosper
and you will
be ready, flesh is
heavy. Spirit for
fortunes, word comes
to us. This is
revelation, and
they could not
take it. Not even
this.

Hangover

It is about
love, it is
about being
surprised. To be
and endure all
things. Common
sense, not allowed
in Love and War.
And patience is
a muscle.

To be or not
not to be
it is all about
in spite of everything
and do not give up
said to many
times. Word without
action is
death.

Rednecks and square heads
everyone lives together
fulfill your race
to destroy. Nothing is
enough to make
a war, proudness
kills humbleness
like an eagle
in thin air
with a big
vision.

Ego

Now it is I
who decides.
Shirt and tie
and someone say:
Wagon and driver's license
please.

Who knows
it could have been
me.

Headache
prolapse and everything
are shadows from
a childhood, in
aesthetic form
far away from
anger and forgiveness

Who knows
it could have been
me.

And the sophist
took maturity
in me
seriously, as
understanding
and have made me
to playroom for
wonder and conviction
climate change and
old age.

Who knows
it could have been
you.

The land of Magog

(A people in the far far north.)

You will find them
in cyberspace
beyond the north wind
which cold is
a language
and:
God is dead

Collection on Armageddon
and the enemy is
oneself.
Attacks are the best
defense
telepathy has
gone out on
fashion, and Geiger counter
which turns out
everything.

In the distance
I see everything
and revelations
is more than enough.

And the dark side
of us
just became
a philosophical thesis.

Bible

(In all its simplicity.)

After the Fall of Man
but before Darwin
we became like the animals.
The similarity has
a developmental learning from
the fall of a dropout
to what was indeed
created very well.

Biting, scratching and everything is
mine, the similarity is limited
until before we get into
the foot of the Sinai mountain
no one dares to climb.

To see God has his
limitations; we want
rather back
to Egypt, like the world
is full of.

In intellectual theory
of evolution
we sail away from
all simplicity
which we are not
able to understand.

Born again

It involves
to be
everything else
than the same
as before.

To bend
and bowed into
clay, soil
and sand.
Stalled from
what is old.
See, everything is new.

Grounded on rock
in a basic form
of solid mass.

My biochemical
life, side effects
in a mass.
Of sand
soil and clay
everything is visible
and receive is
all that is needed.

Then we will let it
be
and live
in the same
for ease of sake.

Biochemical

Cellulose
refined sugar.
From poppy to
morphine and heroin.
And additives
made for duration
and long live
expiration date.

Acidification muddle
everything, except
the proof of
existence.
We can do everything
and do not do anything.

Reflex from
Prima donnas sat
on the tip
in all that is little.

And biochemical me
with my cap in hand
waiting for more
than the world has
to give.

Epilogue

Behold, I stand at the door and knock.
If anyone hears My voice and opens the door,
I will come in to him
and dine with him,
and he with Me.

Revelation 3.20

www.ingramcontent.com/pod-product-compliance
Lightning Source LLC
Chambersburg PA
CBHW060808050426
42449CB00008B/1593

A SKETCH

OF

THE WATERLOO CAMPAIGN:

A SHORT TACTICAL STUDY FOR
YOUNG OFFICERS.

TO WHICH IS ADDED

THE DUKE OF WELLINGTON'S DESPATCH

BY

MAJOR SEYMOUR CLARKE,

Cameron Highlanders.

The Naval & Military Press Ltd

Published by

The Naval & Military Press Ltd

Unit 5 Riverside, Brambleside
Bellbrook Industrial Estate
Uckfield, East Sussex
TN22 1QQ England

Tel: +44 (0)1825 749494

www.naval-military-press.com
www.nmarchive.com